T0395492

SNAILS

ARE JUST MY
SPEED!

A TOON BOOK BY
KEVIN McCLOSKEY

For Brian, my youngest brother and oldest friend.

Editorial Director & Designer: FRANÇOISE MOULY

Guest Editor: RICHARD KUTNER

KEVIN McCLOSKEY's artwork was painted with acrylic paint on parchment-style paper.

SNAILS LIVE IN SHELLS.

THEY MOVE VERY, VERY SLOWLY...

Wait up, you guys!

I'm almost 300 times faster than you, little snail!

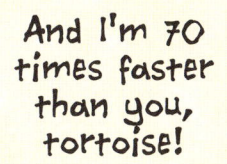

And I'm 70 times faster than you, tortoise!

I'm 4 times faster than a squirrel!

I'm almost twice as fast as a pigeon!

Me, I'm 50 times faster than a SNAIL!

IT CAN BE GOOD TO BE SLOW.
ANIMALS SEE THEIR PREY WHEN IT MOVES.

What eats snails?

HEDGEHOGS

SALAMANDERS

SNAILS BUILD ROADS OF SLIMY MUCUS.

10

THEY FOLLOW ONE ANOTHER'S TRAILS...

AND THEY LIKE TO EAT TOGETHER.

SNAILS MAKE A LOT OF MUCUS.

Mucus is my sunscreen.

WITH MUCUS, THEY CAN TRAVEL ON ANY SURFACE.

I can climb over a knife and not get hurt!

14

Yes, but I can repair it with mucus glue.

YUCK! That's enough about mucus!

AMAZING SNAILS LIVE EVERYWHERE ON EARTH: AT THE BOTTOM OF THE SEA...

AND HIGH UP IN THE MOUNTAINS.

THERE ARE HAIRY SNAILS IN THE RAIN FOREST.

GLASS SNAILS HAVE A SEE-THROUGH SHELL.

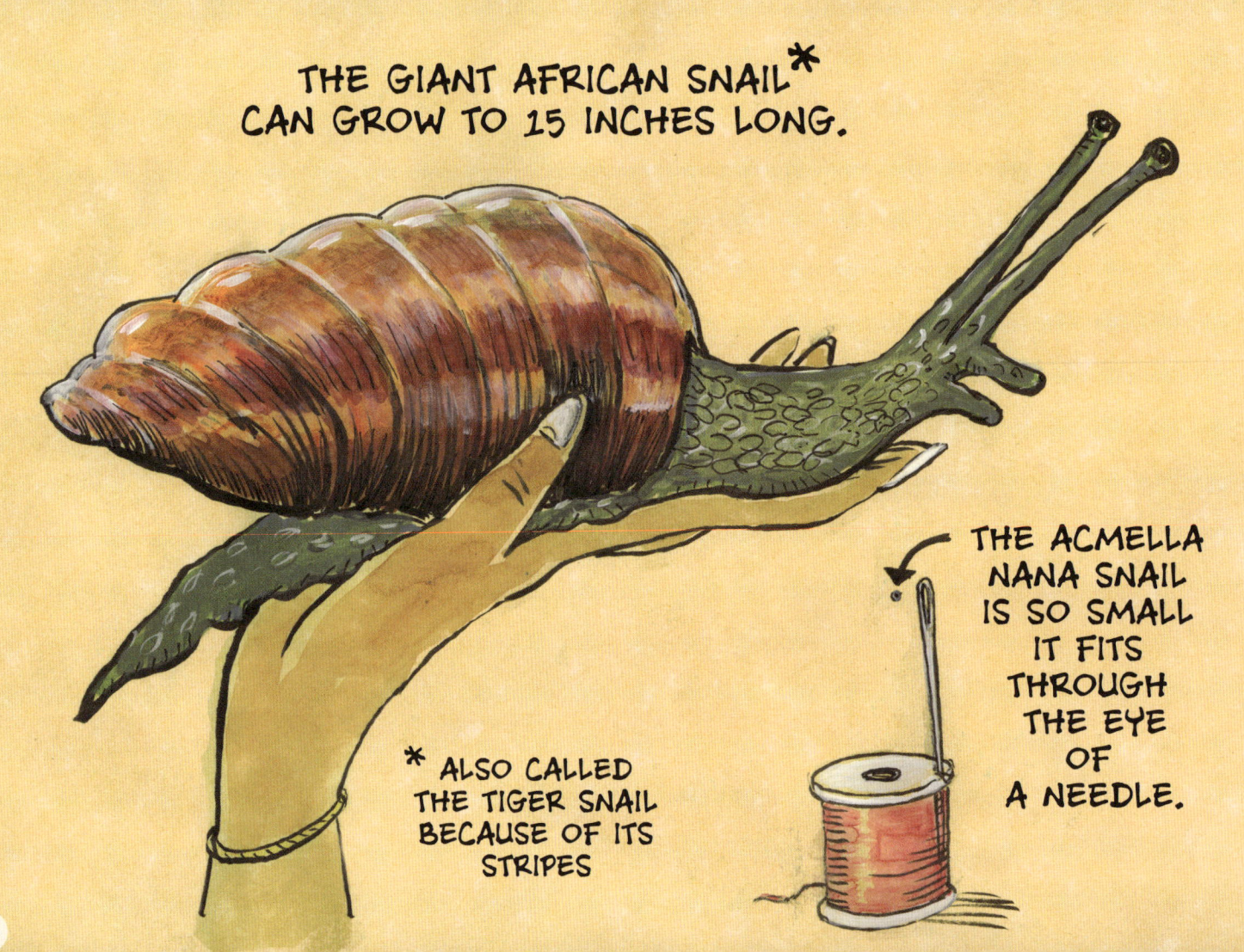

THE GIANT AFRICAN SNAIL*
CAN GROW TO 15 INCHES LONG.

THE ACMELLA NANA SNAIL IS SO SMALL IT FITS THROUGH THE EYE OF A NEEDLE.

* ALSO CALLED THE TIGER SNAIL BECAUSE OF ITS STRIPES

A SNAIL'S TONGUE CAN HAVE OVER 14,000 TEETH!

IT'S LIKE A GRATER OR A FILE.

25

EVEN THE COMMON GARDEN SNAIL IS AMAZING.

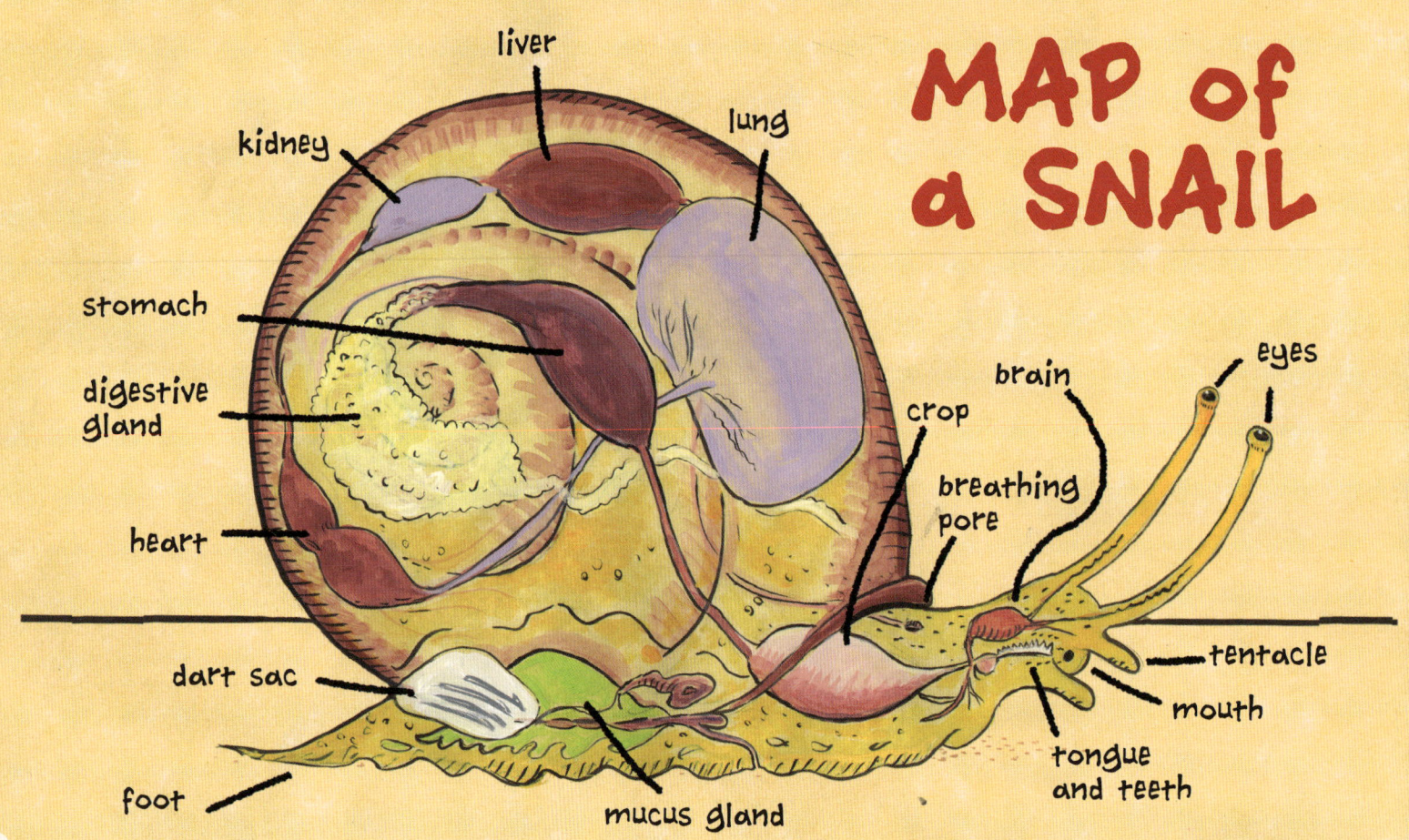

MAP of a SNAIL

liver

lung

kidney

stomach

digestive gland

heart

dart sac

foot

mucus gland

crop

brain

breathing pore

eyes

tentacle

mouth

tongue and teeth

A SNAIL'S EYES ARE WEAK, BUT IT USES ITS LOWER TENTACLES TO FEEL AND SMELL.

THERE ARE THOUSANDS OF KINDS OF SNAILS AND MANY MORE TYPES OF SLUGS. SLUGS ARE SNAILS WITHOUT SHELLS.

EVERY SNAIL IS BOTH MALE AND FEMALE.

That's my Mommy!

That's my Daddy!

SO WE ARE SISTERS

—AND BROTHERS.

THE STORY OF CUPID'S ARROWS MAY HAVE COME FROM SNAILS' "LOVE DARTS."

MONKS OFTEN DREW FIGHTING SNAILS IN OLD BOOKS.

The End is near!

...SNAILS ARE FUN TO DRAW!

6

Start with a 6.

Circle around a few times.

Close up the shell.

Draw the body and eyes.

Don't forget the mucus!

The trick with snails is to draw...

S-L-O-W-L-Y!

Lovely!

ABOUT THE AUTHOR

KEVIN McCLOSKEY taught illustration at Pennsylvania's Kutztown University. After writing this book, Kevin is practically a snail expert, but he can't tell us whether the snails served in restaurants are tasty—he's never eaten one. What's the closest he's come to trying snails? Kevin says, "Sometimes, when I cook artichokes, I put a clove of garlic in the leaves. Then when they're cooked, I forget I put the garlic in and I think there's a slug in my food."

HOW TO READ COMICS WITH KIDS

Kids love comics! They are naturally drawn to the details in the pictures, which make them want to read the words. Comics beg for repeated readings and let both emerging and reluctant readers enjoy complex stories with a rich vocabulary. But since comics have their own grammar, here are a few tips for reading them with kids:

GUIDE YOUNG READERS: Use your finger to show your place in the text, but keep it underneath the character who's speaking so it doesn't hide the very important facial expressions.

HAM IT UP! Think of the comic book story as a play, and don't hesitate to read with expression and intonation. Assign parts or get kids to supply the sound effects, a great way to reinforce phonics skills.

LET THEM GUESS. Comics provide lots of context for the words, so emerging readers can make informed guesses. Like jigsaw puzzles, comics ask readers to make connections, so check a young audience's understanding by asking, "What's this character thinking?" (But don't be surprised if a kid finds some of the comics' subtle details faster than you.)

TALK ABOUT THE PICTURES. Point out how the artist paces the story with pauses (silent panels) or speeded-up action (a burst of short panels). Discuss how the size and shape of the panels convey meaning.

ABOVE ALL, ENJOY! There is of course never one right way to read, so go for the shared pleasure. Once children make the story happen in their imagination, they have discovered the thrill of reading, and you won't be able to stop them. At that point, just go get them more books—and more comics!

www.TOON-BOOKS.com

SEE OUR FREE ONLINE CARTOON MAKERS, LESSON PLANS, AND MUCH MORE